Elijah

*Confrontation, Conflict,
and Crisis*

by

HOWARD G. HENDRICKS

MOODY PRESS

CHICAGO

CONTENTS

1

ELIJAH IN CONFRONTATION

HAVE YOU EVER WONDERED why there is so much in the Scriptures that is biographical? It is obvious to even a casual reader of this Book that its pages are penetrated with personality—men and women who are not fugitives from a wax museum but who are made of the same tissue of life as each of us. The Holy Spirit loves to teach truth in terms of life.

Spiritual biographies leave us in admiration. I cannot come away from the life of a man like Abraham, Moses, Barnabas, or Paul without my spiritual tongue hanging out. I know some say, "You can lead a horse—or a person—to water, but you can't make him drink." That's right. But you can feed him salt. And the lives of these men in the Scriptures is the salt that the Spirit often uses to make us hungry and thirsty for righteousness.

A study of the Word of God in biographical form also leaves us reproved. If you want to know the real poverty of your spiritual life, look into the mirror of the Word. I come away from the study of a man like Abraham and think, If he did what he did with what he had, what should I be doing on the basis of what I have?

Studying biblical biographies leaves us without excuse. I find it tears away every excuse which I palm off to God as a reason why I am not living more effectively for Him.

But in the fourth place, such a study leaves us with hope. Don't say, "It can't be done." They did it.

Some years ago I had a deacon in my church who was the reincarnation of Peter. Every week that went by, I was more convinced that Peter had returned in the flesh. In a Bible class I had a series on the life of Peter, and I brought the series to a climax by using that thumbnail sketch our Lord penned of the apostle Peter in John 1:42: "Thou art Simon . . . thou shalt be called Cephas, which is by interpretation, A stone." The before and the after. When I got to the end, everybody got up and walked out except this man. He sat directly in front of me with his head cupped in his hands, looking directly at me. Finally he said, "Preacher, I've got it. I said, "You've got what, Jack?" "I've got it. If God can do something for Peter, He can do something for me." God the Spirit was coming through loud and clear in terms of an individual with whom this man could identify.

In this book, I would like to direct your attention to five selected episodes in the life of Elijah. First, we want to see Elijah in confrontation. Verse 1 of 1 Kings 17 says, "And Elijah the Tishbite, who was of the inhabitants of Gilead, said unto Ahab, As the LORD God of Israel liveth, before whom I stand, there shall not be dew nor rain these years, but according to my word." He storms up the palace steps, into the presence of the king, and declares his ultimatum. I think I overhear two of the secret service men. One says to the other, "Hey! Where did he come from? How did he get in here?" And while they're discussing the matter, Elijah has disappeared.

Whence such courage? You will never understand nor appreciate what Elijah did until you understand the times in which he lived. The nation was on the skids. The spiritual horizon was dreadfully monotonous. There was a mania of mediocrity. Seven thousand believers were huddled miserably in a cave in silent protest: "We don't want to get involved." This man, Elijah, stands out like a spiritual colossus in the midst of a generation of spiritual pygmies and perverts. Chapter 16 tells the sad story of the rapid spread and universal prevalence of idolatry. It comes to a climax in verses 30-33, where we read,

> And Ahab the son of Omri did evil in the sight of the LORD above all that were before him. And it came to pass, as if it had been a light thing for him to walk in the sins of Jeroboam the son of Nebat, that he took to wife Jezebel, the daughter of Ethbaal king of the Zidonians, and went and served Baal, and worshipped him. And he reared up an altar for Baal in the house of Baal, which he had built in Samaria. And Ahab made a grove; and Ahab did more to provoke the LORD God of Israel to anger than all the kings of Israel that were before him.

It was not convenient nor comfortable to take a stand for God in that generation. It never is. What is the secret of a man or a woman communicating with a generation of chaos? May I underscore in your thinking three keys, three secrets, to the effective communication of this man in his generation and to effective communication in our generation?

In the first place, Elijah was convinced of the reality of Jehovah. "As the LORD God of Israel liveth. . . ." He's alive. Ahab and those confederate with him thought they had successfully enbalmed and interred Jehovah-worship. But they made one serious miscalculation: they forgot a man. And that's all it takes in any generation with the living God—one man overwhelmed by His aliveness, shot through with the reality that only God can bring into human experience.

The most convincing thing about Christianity is its power to change men. The world is not overwhelmed by your argumentation. The world is not overwhelmed by your success story. The world is convinced only by that which it cannot produce—that is reality in human experience. Only God can produce that. That's why Christianity is the most revolutionary thing in all the world; it promises to revolutionize people. You can never change society until you change the most important person in that society, the individual.

What is there in your life that you cannot explain on any basis other than the supernatural? What is there in your life that is proof positive of the reality of God in your life? So you believe God is alive. Why, there's not an unbeliever in a carload. I didn't ask you if you believed that. I asked you what changes are being wrought in your experience today that are proof positive to a world screaming for reality that God is alive?

It is amazing how difficult it is for the Lord to break through to us in certain areas. I used to pray for years as a father, "Lord, change my children." And nothing happened. I used to go into my study at the seminary and throw myself across the desk and say, "O Lord, overhaul my students." And nothing happened.

Then I began to see that my prayer must be changed: "Lord, change my children's father. Change my students' professor." And when God was pleased to do that, I saw remarkable, dramatic changes in my children and in my students.

Some years ago I was to speak at a banquet on a Friday night and then the following morning catch a plane for a weekend ministry. As I came home from the seminary and drove into the driveway, my headlights fell upon my boy's bicycle tire—flat as a doornail. I knew it was either now or never; so, I plowed in and we fixed Bob's bicycle tire. I got washed up and tore across town and got there about twenty minutes late to the banquet.

The emcee had ulcers on his ulcers by the time I got there.

"Where in the world have you been?" "I'm awfully sorry," I said. "I had a flat." He said, "I thought you had a new car." "I do," I answered. "It was my boy's bicycle tire." Boom! This man's cork went off, and quite frankly he gave me a portion of his mind I don't really think he could afford to lose. After he got through, I said to him (graciously, I hope), "Did it ever occur to you, my friend, that on certain occasions it is far more important that I fix my boy's bicycle tire than that I eat your meal?"

Sometime later my boy and I were out in the park playing ball together, and then we took a little walk through a wooded section. We stopped under a tree and were throwing some stones into a creek and I asked him, "Hey, Bob, do you love me?" He said, "I sure do, Dad." "Great. Why?" "Why? I don't know." How philosophic can you get for eight? "Bob," I told him, "you never want to love anybody or anything without having a reason." Quite frankly, I forgot all about it. It must have been a half hour later; he spun around and said, "Hey, Dad! I've got a reason!" I said, "A reason for what?" "Why I love you." "Oh," I said. "Wonderful, pal. Why?" He said, "Because you play ball with me and fix my bicycle tire." Did you ever have the Lord pick up a two-by-four and drop it right on the center of your head?

My children are not impressed by the fact that I'm a seminary professor. Imagine that! My youngest boy sometime ago asked me, "When are you gonna get a new job?" I said, "What's the matter? Don't you like my job" "Naw." "Why not?" "Aw, I can't explain to anybody where you work. They all think you work in a cemetery." No, my kids are not impressed by all the religious routine in which I'm engaged. They're not impressed by my knowledge of the original languages. They're not impressed by the words that neatly and easily cascade from my lips. They are impressed by the reality of Jesus Christ in my life. It would be easy to pull the wool over your eyes in this book but it's not easy to pull the wool over the eyes of my wife and four teenage kids in the city of Dallas. They know whether I have the real disease or not.

How do you convince a world that God is alive? By His aliveness in your life, by His work in producing reality in your experience. What a message for a phony generation.

I want you to notice a second truth in this man's experience that I believe the Spirit of God wants to weave into the pattern of ours. Not only was Elijah convinced of the reality of Jehovah, he was also convinced that he was a representative of the living God: "As the LORD God of Israel liveth, before whom I stand. . . ." My friends, that gives dignity to Christian experience. I never cease to be amazed that God can consistently perform the miracle of the ministry, and that is to employ human personality to accomplish His purpose. I am a personal representative of the living God.

In the midst of a generation where the world is screaming for answers, Christians are stuttering. Christians are paralyzed. Christians are uninvolved in the process of giving the only answer to the searching questions which men are asking. And I know many Christians are asking, "What can I do?" I am quite sure that Elijah could have come to the same conclusion: The nation is headed for doom. The moral microbes are eating the heart out of it. Over here in a cave, seven thousand who can't speak.

It is still true, as in Elijah's time, that God is looking for one man, one woman, who will become His personal representative. Behind the pulpit? Certainly. In a classroom in a Bible school? By all means. Through varied forms of Christian work? To be sure. But also in communities, in homes, in offices, in shops, on university and college and high school campuses, where people who are blind to the glories of our Christ see Him incarnate in you, His personal representative.

My spiritual experience has been revolutionized recently. I must confess, as many a Christian worker must, that it's very easy to become compulsively active. It is hard to learn the lesson of the barrenness of busyness. Your activity simply becomes an anesthetic to deaden the pain of an empty life. And if you get off long enough, you discover you have activity without accomplishment. I used to get up every morning with the compulsiveness of a Christian: "I've got to go to work today. I've got to witness today. I've got to do this and that today." I was quite active, but there was a sterility about my experience. Then the truth dawned on me that all God wanted me to be was available—His messenger boy, a suit of clothes in His ready-to-wear department that He could put on at will to accomplish His purpose.

I had just finished a week of meetings in which I had spoken thirty-four times in eight days, and I was flying from Chicago to Los Angeles. I had to change planes in Denver, and by the time I got there, I was very weary. When I got on the plane, I went all the way to the back—third seat in— hoping no one would come and sit by me. "Lord, don't send anyone here. Your servant has been so busy." The plane filled up and nobody sat there, until finally the only seat left was the one next to me. A man got on the plane, came down the aisle, sat down next to me, took out his little executive case, opened it, and then with expletives I shall not repeat, shouted, "Where is my brief? I'm on my way to try a case in Los Angeles and I don't have the brief." He got up, tore down the aisle, and told the stewardess, "You've got to open that door. I've got to get out of here." So they went through all the pains of opening the door.

Sitting outside, now completely exhausted and partially

asleep, was a GI who had been bumped nineteen times in a row—and this was the nineteenth. The agent said, "Hey, buddy, you're on." He never got the message. He told me later they had to almost pick him up and put him on the plane. And this boy came down the aisle and sat next to me.

I thought, *Lord, I hope he's not talkative.* He was incurably takative. Finally, in the midst of the conversation, he asked, as invariably someone will, "By the way, mister, what do you do?"

This is always embarrassing, you know. I usually make good progress in a conversation until finally somebody asks, "Oh, by the way, what do you do?" "Well, I'm in education." "Oh, that's very interesting. Where do you teach?" "Well, I teach at the Dallas Theological Seminary." "The what? Oh, yeah! I get it, you're a preacher!" You see, those of us who are preachers are paid to be good. The rest of you are good for nothing.

This time I didn't fudge. I said, "Son, I'm a preacher." He said, "Really?" I said, "Really." He said, "Mister, I'm on my way to Vietnam. I know I'm not supposed to be, but I'm scared to death. You got anything that would help me?"

So I got my Testament out and explained the gospel to him, and somewhere between Denver and Los Angeles, he accepted Christ as his Saviour. I said, "Now, friend, I want you to do me a favor. I'm going to write my name and address on this card. When you get to Vietnam, I want you to drop me a note, and I'll send you some literature that'll help you build on this foundation."

So this guy got to Vietnam, and when he walked into the barracks, the sergeant said, "Hey, buddy. You new around here?" "That's right, sir." He said, "OK, I want you to get the signals straight. Tomorrow's Sunday, and in this outfit everybody goes to chapel. That includes you. Right?" "Yes, sir."

So Sunday he went to chapel, and the chaplain got up and preached the gospel. The kid thought, *You know, that's the same thing that guy talked about on the plane.* So after the service he went up to talk to the chaplain. "Hey, chaplain, you know, an amazing thing happened. I was flying from Denver to Los Angeles and a man told me the very message you were talking about and I received Jesus Christ as my Saviour. In fact, he said that if I'd write to him, he'd send me some literature. Here's his name." And the chaplain said, "That was my professor at Dallas Seminary."

A lot of people would say, "Isn't that an interesting story? Isn't that filled with concidences?" A lawyer just happened to forget his brief; a kid just happened to be bumped nineteen times in a row; he just happened to sit down next to me; he just happened to ask if I could help him with his fear; he just happened to land in Vietnam, and of all the places, in a group where there was a believing chaplain who preached the Word of God and got him in a Bible class so that he could grow. I don't believe that any of this was coincidence at all. I believe this is a part of the excitement of waking up every day to say, "Lord, I'm simply Your suit of clothes. Put me on to accomplish Your purpose."

I want you to see one final truth. Elijah was not only convinced of the reality of Jehovah and that he was a personal representative of that God to his generation; but he was also convinced of the resources which were available to him.

We need to do some reconstructing of the text, and in the book of James you will find a divine commentary on this passage. In James 5:17 we are told something that we know nothing about in 1 Kings: "Elias [Elijah] was a man subject to like passions as we are, and he prayed earnestly that it might not rain: and it rained not on the earth by the space of three years and six months." This man's courage to confront the king and his generation was the product of his prayer life. But where did he get the idea to pray like that? Two verses in Deuteronomy 11 give us a clue, I think: "Take heed to yourselves, that your heart be not deceived, and ye turn aside, and serve other gods, and worship them; and then the LORD's wrath be kindled against you, and he shut up the heaven, that there be no rain, and that the land yield not her fruit; and lest ye perish quickly from off the good land which the LORD giveth you" (vv. 16-17). It is my personal conviction that Elijah knew that what God had promised, He was able also to perform. He knew that God had promised that if a nation defected spiritually, He would withhold the rain. This man prayed earnestly that what God had promised, He would also perform.

So often people ask me, "What can I do? What resources are available to me in the midst of this apostasy?" Elijah did not have one thing that is not completely available to everyone reading this book. He had the Word of God. He had the power of prayer. What more do you need? The ability to believe God for what He says and then to appropriate it by believing prayer. It is one thing to believe the Lord, to know that He can do it, but it's quite a different thing to appropriate it in your experience.

I did something last summer I do not believe I have ever done before in my life. I hope I never have to do it again. I was in a prayer meeting made up just of pastors, and the unbelief was so crass I had to get up and walk out. I went back to my room and got the Word out and filled myself with the living God until I realized afresh that I am His representative in this generation and that all the resources available to any other individual of faith are completely available to me.

There are too many black crepes hung on doors of Christian hearts, too many unbelievers among us. Please note, I did not say unsaved but unbelievers. Oh, for the capacity to stretch ourselves out upon an infinite God and to believe Him to do what He specializes in: the impossible.

2

ELIJAH IN CONCEALMENT

CHAD WALSH wrote an intriguing book entitled *Early Christians of the Twenty-first Century*, in which he placed a burr in my mental saddle with these words: "Millions of Christians live in a sentimental haze of vague piety, with soft organ music trembling in the lovely light from stained glass windows. Their religion is a pleasant thing of emotional quivers, divorced from the will, divorced from the intellect and demanding little except lip service to a few harmless platitudes. I suspect that Satan has called off his attempt to convert people to agnosticism. After all, if a man travels far enough away from Christianity, he is liable to see it in perspective and decide that it is true. It is much safer, from Satan's point of view, to vaccinate a man with a mild case of Christianity so as to protect him from the real disease."

There is nothing as repulsive as phoniness in the spiritual realm. Conversely there is nothing as magnetic as reality. How refreshing to study the life of a man (Elijah) who was for real. There is not a shred of phoniness in this man's life and experience. Problems? Yes. Phoniness? No.

In the last chapter we focused our attention on 1 Kings 17:1, which constitutes an introduction to the life of the prophet. There we saw Elijah in confrontation. This rustic renegade from the rural regions storms into the palace of the king and delivers his ultimatum. He was able to communicate in a generation of spiritual declension because he was convinced of the reality of God—God was alive. He was also convinced that he was God's personal representative to that society, and that created responsibility, a responsibility to speak when others were hiding. Further, he was convinced that there were resources adequate and available. And the Word of God had become his word. He had laid hold of the throne of God in prayer, that it might not rain, and it rained not.

Now we turn from Elijah in confrontation to a study of Elijah in concealment. And there is a cause-effect relationship. You show me an individual who is effective in public, and I will show you an individual who is effective in private. You show me an individual who is communicating with his generation spiritually, and I will show you a man who is communicating with his God. We like the assignment of confrontation, but the assignment of concealment is hard to choke down.

May I encourage you to write four words in the margin of your Bible? These four words unravel the plot of 1 Kings 17:2-7. First of all, besides verses 2 and 3 write "command." Beside verse 4 write "promise"; beside verses 5 and 6, "response"; and beside verse 7, "test." The order is both significant and spiritual: a command, a promise, a response, and a test. Let's examine these in detail.

In verses 2 and 3, note the command: "And the word of the LORD came unto him, saying, Get thee hence, and turn thee eastward, and hide thyself by the brook Cherith, that is before Jordan." "Hide myself, Lord? When there's so much to be done, and so few people involved in doing it? Hide myself?" Go show yourself. That's easy. Go hide thyself. That's difficult. I'm sure, had I been in Elijah's place, I would have remonstrated with the Lord. "Lord, are You sure the IBM card is not crumpled? Lord, are You sure Your PBX operator does not have the wrong plug in? Lord, I'm a palace man. And You want a palace man to hide himself?"

I am convinced that there are many Christians today to whom God is saying incisively, "Go hide yourself." That is a difficult assignment in a busy world. We are compulsive activists, and there are so many voices clamoring for our attention that it is easy to miss the voice of God in the process. You may be asking God to use you, to shape you, to mold you, to give you a cutting edge, not only in the present generation but, if the Lord tarries, in the next generation. But you will have nothing to say to this generation or the next unless God first speaks to you. The important thing is not what you read or what you hear in a school or in a conference from an individual who is simply an instrument in the hands of God. In the final analysis, the important thing is whether you hear from God Himself. And if you do not hear from Him, then all that those men and women may tell you will not make sense, nor will it have its designed impact.

At a pastors' conference some time ago I talked to a man who came to see me for counsel. He had severe problems in his work. I asked, "Pastor, how much time do you spend thinking?" "Thinking? Hendricks, I don't have any time to think. If I stop to think, I get behind." And this is precisely our dilemma.

Julian the Apostate during the first century was determined to blot out every trace of Christianity. He discovered to his embarrassment the law of spiritual thermodynamics—the greater the heat, the greater the expansion. The more he persecuted Christianity, the more it flourished. Finally he gathered his little straggling band of men in an upper room and shouted to them, "Bah! Christianity provokes too much thinking. Why, even the slaves are thinking." This, to a Roman mind, was incredible, because, said the Romans, slaves do not think. But slaves do think under the impact of the Word. Do you? I have never met a Christian who sat down and planned to live a mediocre life. But if you keep going in the direction in which you are moving, you may land there. The unexamined life is not worth living. How we need to hear in our giddy age, "Go hide thyself."

Now note, in verse 4, the promise. God never gives a command without providing the dynamic to fulfill that command. He never calls you to a task without providing all the resources you need for it. "And it shall be, that thou shalt drink of the brook; and I have commanded the ravens to feed thee there." Very simple fare, but sufficient.

I have had wonderful opportunities working with students. A student who comes to see me periodically now is a young man dreaming dreams and seeing visions. If I can just keep him away from some older Christians who want to throw a wet blanket on what God is leading him to do, you're going to hear from this young man in the next generation. If I were to tell you what he is planning, many of you would laugh, so absurd appears to be the idea right now. But he feels God is leading him to it, he has been planning and thinking and praying. He came to see me not too long ago and said, "Prof, there are a lot of problems. God's going to have to do a miracle work if we ever get this off the ground."

I said, "That's what God specializes in. Did it ever occur to you that there is not a work of God in our day that has not been the product of a miracle-working God?" I reminded this boy of the experience of Dallas Seminary.

Shortly after the seminary was founded in 1924, it almost capitulated. It came to the point of bankruptcy. All the creditors were going to foreclose at twelve noon on a particular day. That morning the founders of the school met in the president's office to pray that God would provide. And in that prayer meeting was Harry Ironside. When it was his turn to pray, he prayed in his characteristically refreshing manner: "Lord, we know that the cattle on a thousand hills are Thine. Please sell some of them and send us the money."

While they were praying, a tall Texan with boots on and an open collar came into the business office and said, "I just sold two carloads of cattle in Fort Worth. I've been trying to make a business deal go through and it won't work, and I feel God is compelling me to give this money to the seminary. I don't know if you need it or not, but here's the check." A little secretary took the check and, knowing something of the criticalness of the hour financially, went to the door of the prayer meeting and timidly tapped. When she finally got a response, Dr. Chafer took the check out of her hand, and it was for the exact amount of the debt. When he looked at the signature on the check, he recognized the name of the cattleman from Fort Worth. Turning to Dr. Ironside, he said, "Harry, God sold the cattle."

I have read enough of the history of Moody Bible Institute to know that this school stands today as the product of and as a monument to a miracle-working God. As long as this school, or any other school or work, is faithful to the commands of God, He will supply. And when any institution or other work of God begins to waver and move away from His commands, it will go broke.

Are you also dreaming dreams and seeing visions? Is the Spirit of God moving in your life with concern to reach the thousands of people who couldn't care less about Jesus Christ? Let me introduce you to the God Elijah knew by intimacy, the God who said, "Go hide yourself," and who also said, "I'll feed you. I'll give you drink."

Next we come to two verses which, I must confess, my heart leaps to because they are so in contrast to my own experience. Verses 5 and 6 tell of the response of this man of God. There was the command and then the promise. But there must be a response. "So he went and did according unto the word of the LORD: for he went and dwelt by the brook Cherith, that is before Jordan. And the ravens brought him bread and flesh in the morning, and bread and flesh in the evening; and he drank of the brook."

I mentioned earlier that if I had been in Elijah's place, I would have been conducting an argument with God. You know, there is a lot of humor in the Scriptures, and Acts 9 contains one of the most human of the incidents.

As the chapter opens, we are introduced to the early church's public enemy number one—Saul. "Breathing out threatenings and slaughter," he is moving from Jerusalem to Damascus when on the road he meets the risen Christ and is revolutionized. In verse 26 we read, "And when Saul was come to Jerusalem, he assayed [or attempted] to join himself to the disciples: but they were all afraid of him, and believed not that he was a disciple." I think I overhear one of them saying, "Look, how sharp can you get? This man feigns conversion in order to get on the inside of the group and find out who are identified with the group, and then he'll proceed to liquidate us one by one. Oh, no. We're not taking him in." It is hard for me to believe this in terms of contemporary Christianity. We open the doors of the church and the people come forward and we ask them profound questions, such as, "You know Jesus Christ as your Saviour, don't you?" If they have half a brain cell functioning, they know how to answer. So when I read a section like this, I find it very difficult to identify.

Beginning at verse 10 of the same chapter we can get a

little flash of insight as to why they were skeptical of Saul's conversion: "And there was a certain disciple at Damascus, named Ananias; and to him said the Lord in a vision, Ananias. And he said, Behold, I am here, Lord. And the Lord said unto him, Arise . . . ." "Yes, sir." ". . . and go into the street which is called Straight . . . ." "Roger." ". . . and enquire in the house of Judas . . . ." "Got it." ". . . for one called Saul of Tarsus."

I don't think Ananias heard a word from here on out. How do I know? He prayed, and in his prayer he proceeded to give God a little information. Did you ever do that in your praying? Look at verse 13: "Lord, I have heard by many of this man, how much evil he hath done to thy saints [and I'm one of them] at Jerusalem: and here he hath authority from the chief priests to bind all that call on thy name."

Now I know you have a period in your text, but I do not believe there should be a period here. I don't think Ananias ever finished his prayer. God interrupted: "Go thy way. . . ." For a moment when God said to Ananias, "Go," he argued, "Lord, are You apprised of all the facts?" But here when God said, "Go thy way," he ceased debating. And he went and put his hands on Saul (v. 17) and called him Brother Saul. How would you like his assignment? How would you like to put your hands on public enemy number one, recently converted? You would not be sure but what this man might get up from his knees and put air between your head and your body.

In 1 Kings 17 when God tells Elijah, who had been so successful in the spectacularly dramatic ministry in the palace, "Go hide yourself," there is not a word of debate or argument. "He went and did according unto the word of the LORD." The opposite of ignorance in the spiritual realm is not knowledge, it is obedience. "To obey is better than sacrifice, and to hearken than the fat of rams" (1 Sa 15:22). The Lord and I have a running argument. I constantly attempt to impress Him with how much I know. He constantly seeks to impress me with how little I have obeyed. Elijah goes to the Cherith Bible Conference, and he is served typical Bible conference fare: bread and flesh in the morning; bread and flesh in the evening!

Now turn to verse 7—the test: "And it came to pass after a while, that the brook dried up." What a revolting development! "Lord, didn't You tell me to come here?" "Right." "How can I be in the center of Your will and have a drying brook?" My friends, God is not simply interested in the impartation of your faith; He is interested in the development of your faith. And He knows that faith only develops under pressure, it only develops in the crucible.

God called Abraham out of Ur of the Chaldees, across the Fertile Crescent, and down into the land. He no sooner arrived in the center of the will of God, the place of plenty, and there was a severe famine. The first thing he did was head for Egypt, and what a pack of trouble he got into.

I see some thrilling testimonies of the leadership of the Lord in the life of our seminary students. Here is a young college man, extremely gifted, well trained, who graduates and goes into a professional field where he is eminently successful. Every time he turns around he receives another advancement. But spiritually he is fed up. "This isn't it. There's no fulfillment here for me." He feels the call of God upon his life, and he resigns his position and sells his house. God has called him to train for vocational Christian work and he lands in Dallas. At the end of the third week of his first semester he surveys the scene. He still has no job. He is beginning to think he is highly qualified to be utterly useless. His wife is sick. And furthermore, he gets three blue books returned through the mailbox, each one of which has an "F" on it. He doesn't know much Greek yet, but he knows enough English to know that that does not stand for "fine."

I have seen such a student come with these blue books clutched in his hand and stand in my office, and he says, "Prof, what happened? I have never been more convinced that I am directly in the will of God. But I have no job, my wife is sick, and I'm flunking three courses." I have often said, "My friend, this is as much a part of the curriculum God has designed to shape you as the courses in which you are enrolled."

Our Lord illustrates this principle in Mark 4. In this chapter you have a portion of our Saviour's teacher-training program as He attempted to groom a handful of men for a ministry of multiplication. He presented a series of parables which focused on the subject of faith, but He knew that you do not learn faith by lecture, you learn faith in the laboratory of life. Our Lord was a good teacher. He gave examinations, but not the kind we give at the seminary. We give cramming exams, where we test to see how much the student can cram in his bean.

"And the same day [the day in which they had just heard the lectures on faith from the world's greatest teacher], when the even was come, he [the Lord] saith unto them, Let us pass over unto the other side" (v. 35). So they took off across the water. Mark tells us in verse 37: "There arose a great storm of wind, and the waves beat into the ship, so that it was now full." That is his way of telling you they had had it. This was a hopeless case. This was a group of professional fishermen who had spent all their lives on that lake, and they had never seen such a storm. So they came to the Lord, who interestingly enough was asleep in the back part of the boat. To translate it graphically, they said, "Lord, don't

You even care that we're in the process of going down?" The implication is, "At least You can help us bail out." Then the Lord rebuked the wind and the waves, and there was no problem. The wind ceased; there was a great calm.

Then the Lord said to them, "Why are ye so fearful? How is it that ye have no faith?" (v. 40). The little word *ye* is in the emphatic position. "How is it that you, of all people, have no faith, you who just heard the lecture?" They wrote a blue book exam, and it came back with a big "F" on it, and that was not for "faith."

I have asked myself, Suppose Jesus Christ were to return to speak personally to my own, or your own, church congregation? What would He say? Is it possible that with all the graciousness and compassion of His heart, He would turn to us as an audience and say, "How is it that you, of all people, have no faith?" Privilege creates responsibility. Revelation demands response. God has commanded. He has promised. The next step is yours. It is a step of obedience. But mark it well. The moment you take a significant step of obedience, you're going to be put into the crucible, you're going to be tested. You're going to have to write a blue book on your faith.

I am sure many people—perhaps you—are sitting today by a drying brook. It could be financial. It could be physical. It could be intellectual, for those in school. It could be emotional. It could be spiritual. And you're asking, "Lord, what happened?" And He answers, "Nothing. I'm just answering your prayer."

Put yourself in Elijah's position for just a moment. Here he sits and the brook diminishes. It becomes a trickle; then only a few puddles are left; and then even they evaporate. How do you respond to that? I have the highest respect for Elijah. I wouldn't have been able to sit there and watch the brook diminish. I would have gotten out my road map and been looking for every water hole in the area. My motto would be: "Don't sit there. Do something." But Elijah sat by the drying brook, and can you imagine what he must have thought? "How come the brook is drying up? What caused that?" Finally it dawned on him with impact—"The brook is drying up because I prayed that it would." "He [Elijah] prayed earnestly that it might not rain: and it rained not on the earth by the space of three years and six months" (Ja 5:17).

Sometimes you have asked, "Lord, make me like Your Son." And He took you at your word and began the process and you said, "Lord, what happened? Why did You allow this to come into my life? What are You doing with this drying brook?" He answers, "Nothing, except answering your prayer." For never forget, Jesus Christ, "though he were a Son, yet learned he obedience by the things which he suffered" (Heb 5:8).

Perhaps the Spirit of God is saying to many of us today, "I want to minister through you. But before I can ever minister *through* you, I must minister *to* you." Don't despise the educational experience of your drying brook. Don't throw in the towel. Don't perform an abortion upon the divinely devised process. Let patience have her perfect work, that you may be mature and complete. He wants to make you just like His Son.

3

ELIJAH IN CONFLICT

GOD'S METHODS invariably involve a man. But what kind of man does God choose and use? God's choice of material is diametrically opposed to man's. Man chooses an individual on the basis of what he is. God chooses an individual on the basis of what he is to become. When we last saw Elijah, he was sitting by a drying brook, in the process of becoming. God was ministering *to* him. Now He is prepared to minister *through* him.

I suppose there is no more dramatic scene in all Scripture than the contest on Mount Carmel. I wish I were an artist and could render the scene. Two explosive personalities collide, and the moment they do, the sparks fly. Ahab says to Elijah, "Art thou he that troubleth Israel?" (1 Ki 18:17), more literally translated from the original text, "Is it you, you troubler of Israel?" Elijah is equal to the occasion. Like Nathan the prophet, he points his finger and says, *"Thou* art the man." He scores Ahab for his sin and in so doing throws down the gauntlet. There is no question in my mind who is in charge here. Seven times over Elijah takes the initiative. He issues the commands. He issues the initial command—the battle of the gods.

This was a national holiday in Israel. I can see them now, streaming up to the top of that mountain with its commanding view of the Mediterranean Sea. They are coming up by every available route to witness the battle of the gods, fifteen rounds, winner take all. And it is a scene of contrasts. By far the overwhelming majority are gathered over on this side. Here are the eight hundred fifty prophets of Baal and the prophets of the grove, clad in their expensive, beautifully colored garments. Around each neck hangs a piece of metal deliberately designed to catch and reflect the rays of the sun, for they worshiped the sun. Soon that group parts for the grand entry of the king. He is borne by his retinue of servants on a litter. He is resplendently robed as well, with all his regal garments. Then your eye shifts. On the other side is a lone, gaunt man, crudely clothed, coarse in appearance, hair disheveled, eyes like steel. Someone says, "Isn't it a shame? He's so lonely." My friends, don't feel sorry for Elijah, because Elijah does not feel sorry for himself.

Mark in your Bible, or at least underline in your mind, the seven statements of Elijah which unfold the story. It's a familiar story, but through this route we can derive the practical lessons which emerge.

Elijah's first statement is in verse 21. He begins by preaching a clear, concise sermon: "How long halt ye between two opinions?" He scores the people with the sin of indecisiveness. They are at the fork. He says, "You're going to have to make a decision." Elijah would have had no sympathy with the politician who, when asked, "Are you for or against this issue?" replied, "Well, some of my friends are for it. Some of my friends are against it. And I'm for my friends." Elijah is concerned that the people do not emerge from this contest firmly planted in midair. He tells them, "You're going to have to make a choice. You've been straddling the fence, but there is no room for peaceful coexistence. It's either Jehovah or Baal. Make your choice." And in so saying, he stuns them into absolute silence.

He speaks again. In verse 22, he first of all underscores the problem: "I, even I only, remain a prophet of the LORD." And then he makes a proposal: "Call ye on the name of your gods, and I will call on the name of the LORD: and the God that answereth by fire, let him be God" (v. 24). Baal was the chief deity in the Canaanite pantheon. He was the lord of heaven. Whenever it would thunder, whenever they would see lightning flash across the sky, they would exclaim, "That's Baal. That's Baal." He was the lord of fire. If there is anything a god of fire ought to be able to do, it's light a fire. So the people answer, "It is well spoken. That's an equitable arrangement. In fact, it's decidedly to our advantage. We agree."

The third statement is found in verse 25: "You go first," Elijah tells them. "Choose you one bullock for yourselves, and dress it first . . . and call on the name of your gods, but put no fire under." This they do, and all morning they perform their weird dancing around the altar and chant monotonously, "O Baal, hear us." But, we read at the end of verse 26, "there was no voice, nor any that answered"—because, my Bible tells me, false gods have eyes, but they see not; they have ears, but they hear not; they have mouths, but they speak not; they have hands and feet, but they do not move in response to those that call upon them (Ps 115:2-8). There is dreadful silence. And the priests of Baal leap upon the altar.

Then when the sun is at its hottest, when the god they worship is at his zenith, Elijah, his tongue laden with sarcasm, inserts the needle. He had a fantastic sense of humor. This must have been the most enjoyable part of the experience. "It came to pass at noon, that Elijah mocked them, and said, Cry aloud: for he is a god" (v. 27). How ridiculous can you get? If he is a god, he certainly can hear. But cry a little louder. Maybe the batteries in his hearing aid are dead. Or maybe he's talking, and remember, he can't listen to two people at the same time. So don't interrupt him. Or maybe he's "pursuing." And it is interesting to note that this is the word used to translate the process of a man out hunting his food. Maybe he's out collecting something to eat. Or maybe he's on a journey. He's taking a little vacation in Florida. Maybe he's asleep. He had an overdose of Sominex last night and he has to be awakened. These words stir the people into a frenzy: "They cried aloud and cut themselves after their manner with knives and lancets, till the blood gushed out upon them" (v. 28).

Mark this, my friends: If it is sincerity that saves, these people should have been saved. They were the most sincere people in all the world, but they were sincerely wrong. They had the wrong object for their faith, and faith is always determined by its object. Suppose I were to wander around in Chicago looking for some unsuspecting individual and I find a guy and I ask, "Say, friend. Would you fly me to Dallas?" "Dallas," he asks. "Where's that?" "Well, it's south and a little west of here." "Sure, I'll be glad to fly you." So we go out to what is supposed to be a plane. The fuselage is held together with baling wire. It's got just half a prop, and the tail assembly is missing. And I ask him, "By the way, you have been up before, haven't you?" He answers, "No, as a matter of fact, I've never been up before, but I'm fascinated by flying. Hop in." If I would get into that plane with that pilot, it would not be faith, it would be foolishness. Because the object of my faith would be worthless. "There was neither voice, nor any to answer, nor any that regarded" (v. 29).

In verse 30 you have the fourth statement of Elijah. He invites the people, "Come near unto me." That is, "Move in a little closer. I don't want you to think there is any chicanery to my method of procedure. I want you to witness the whole thing." Then he proceeds to repair the altar which had been broken down and to dig a trench.

Then in verse 33 is the fifth statement. He commands, "Fill four barrels with water, and pour it on the burnt-sacrifice, and on the wood." I heard an individual of the liberal persuasion reciting this story, and he stopped at this juncture and said, "Now here is another clear-cut evidence of the inconsistency of the Scripture. They were in the midst of a prolonged drought. There was not enough water to feed the cattle. Men were dying for lack of moisture. And Elijah commands them to fill four barrels of water. Now where would they find that?" And I thought, *This man has forgotten his geography.* Mount Carmel is located beside the Mediterranean Sea. Salt water is bad news for cattle and for men, but it is exquisitely designed for dousing wood.

I think Elijah enjoyed this. "Say, men, run down there to the sea and fill up four barrels," he tells them. Down they go and back they come. They douse the altar. He looks at it. "I really don't think it's wet enough, men. Try it on for size again." So down they go the second time and they come back and saturate it. "It's better, but it's still not good enough. You don't mind making another trip down there, do you?" So down they go again. They come back and everything is one soggy mess. Water is even all around the trench. It is as if Elijah's faith is so great that he would even put obstacles in the way of God.

In verse 36 is his sixth statement. He prayed: "LORD God of Abraham, Isaac, and of Israel. . . ." Note the content of his prayer: "Let it be known this day that thou art God in Israel, and that I am thy servant, and that I have done all of these things at thy word." That sounds like his words to Ahab in 17:1. He prays that these people, like himself, might be convinced of the reality of Jehovah and might realize that Elijah is merely His representative. This prayer is quite a contrast to the prayers of the false prophets that lasted more than six hours. "Hear me, O LORD, hear me, that this people may know that thou art the LORD God, and that thou hast turned their heart back again. Then the fire of the Lord fell and consumed the burnt-sacrifice [no problem here], and the wood [ideal kindling], and the stones . . ." (18:37-38). You know, I've been camping a great deal and I have not found stones to be good kindling; but on Mount Carmel they were consumed as well as the dust. When I want to put a fire out, I use a pail of dust. And it "licked up [evaporated] the water that was in the trench." Seeing this, the people "fell on their faces: and they said, The LORD, he is the God; the LORD, he is the God" (v. 39).

In the morning Baal-worship had prevailed. At the end of this day Jehovah-worship was back in the ascendancy. The last word, the seventh—found in verse 40—is a drastic word, the sentence of judgment. "Take the prophets of Baal; let not one of them escape. And they took them: and Elijah brought them down to the brook Kishon, and slew them there." You say, That's extreme, isn't it? I think not. Remember there was a malignancy in the nation, and this had to be thoroughly excised before there would be any lasting value. Elijah, a spiritual surgeon, knew that, like the surgeon of the body, he had to hurt in order to heal. I think many times we look back with our perverted perspective and sit in judgment without taking into account the effect of sin that is not judged with severity.

I want to underscore for your thinking three principles

which spring from this portion of the Word of God, principles that answer the question, What kind of man does God choose and use?

In the first place, I believe He uses one who is convinced that one plus God constitutes a distinct majority. Divine mathematics are vastly different from human mathematics. We are impressed by numbers, but God is not. We are enamored of addition, God is committed to multiplication. Eight hundred and fifty to one? That's not the equation. It is eight hundred fifty to one *plus God.* And the significance is not the one, but the God who controlled the one.

I love to study the gospels to see how God launched the church. It's conceivable to me that an infinite God could have used an infinite number of means. But why did He launch the church the way He did? I believe it was because this was to become a pattern for our ministry. When you read the gospels, it's obvious that our Lord's paramount ministry was not to the multitudes, who for the most part followed Him for superficial reasons, but to a small band of men, into whose lives He built quality and spiritual impact. In the book of Acts we read that the pagan world testified that these men had "turned the world upside down" (17:6). At the end of Acts we discover that that church, starting with a handful of men, was further toward reaching its world for Christ than we are after these many hundreds of years, with all the methods, with all the technological advances at our disposal. In the spiritual realm, it is never how many, it is always what kind. The question is not, What can we do? The question is, What can God do? "But we're so few." We're overwhelmed by the size of our group rather than by the size of our God. The size of your God will determine the size of everything in your theology and everything in your Christian experience.

One of my favorite pastimes is watching surgery. I have a friend who specializes in microscopic surgery of the middle ear. Some time ago he said, "I want you to see an operation the likes of which you have never seen. It's the most dramatic operation I have performed." They have perfected an operation today in which they keep the patient under partial anesthesia in order to determine the success of the operation. During the surgery the surgeon was looking through one microscope and I was looking through the other. He pointed out two small bones to me. "They are separated and this is the reason this man has not heard for twenty-six years. Now," he said, "I'm going to join these bones and I'm going to continue to speak. And I want you to keep your eyes on his face. If the operation is successful, you'll know it immediately." So I waited with expectancy and sheer excitement. Finally he said, "I'm coming to it now," and he joined the two bones and continued to talk. I watched the man's face. His eyes became like saucers. "What's that? Who's talking?" he said, and tears began to stream down his face. A man who had not heard for twenty-six years was able to hear again. If you and I were going through the human body, examining the component parts, and came upon these two bones—if we could see them—we'd say in our lack of expertise, "Who needs these? They're so small." But size does not determine significance. If you are hearing what I am saying today, it is because those two little bones in your ear, which you probably were never aware of in terms of existence, are properly joined. The problem with most of us is that we are not properly joined to the infinite God. But any believer in proper relationship with Him constitutes a distinct majority, in any situation, in any age.

I want you to notice a second principle here: God uses a man, as He did Elijah, who is not problem-oriented but who is potential-oriented. I'm sure Elijah could have wrung his hands and said, "Things are rough. Seven thousand—but they're in a cave. And I'm on Carmel. What can I do?"

You know, wherever I go, I am interested to see how an individual will tip his hand in the first moments of conversation with me. I spend a lot of time with pastors and Christian workers. Sometimes they pick me up at the airport. I get into the car, and right away they start telling me about their problems. When I ask Christians, "How are you doing?" many answer, "Oh, pretty well—under the circumstances." That is where they spend the bulk of their lives: under the circumstances! Problems are circumstances to which faith has often capitulated. I ran across an interesting statement in my reading the other day: "We are all faced with a series of great opportunities, brilliantly disguised as unsolvable problems." A church that has no problems is probably paralyzed. If you're making progress for God, you have problems. The question is, Where are your eyes?

Numbers 13 records that the children of Israel, wending their way through the wilderness, came to a place called Kadesh Barnea, actually just a wide spot in the road. Here they made a decision that determined their destiny. God told them to go directly into the land, but they said, "Let's not play the part of a fool. Let's be practical. Let's appoint a committee." So in typical committee fashion, they came back with a majority and a minority report. Verse 30 gives the minority report: "And Caleb stilled the people before Moses, and said, Let us go up at once, and possess it; for we are well able to overcome it." He believed they were well able because he believed God was well able. But then the majority gave their report: "But the men that went up with him said, We be not able to go up against the people; for they are stronger than we. And they brought up an evil report of the land

which they had searched unto the children of Israel, saying,
The land, through which we have gone to search it, is a land
that eateth up the inhabitants thereof; and all the people that
we saw in it are men of a great stature. And there we saw
the giants, the sons of Anak, which come of the giants: and
we were in our own sight as grasshoppers, and so we were
in their sight" (vv. 31-33).

Probably every child enrolled in your Sunday school can
give you the names of the two men who brought the minority
report. I defy you to give the name of even one of the ten
men who brought the majority report. They are all found in
the opening verses of chapter 13, but who wants to remember
them? In America we often say, "The majority is always
right." Really? The majority is frequently flat wrong. What
was the difference between these two groups? I believe the
majority was problem-oriented. "We've got giants—red-
wood variety, Texas-size. Besides, we're just a bunch of God's
grasshoppers." What was the difference in Joshua and Caleb?
They had seen the giants too. And I don't think they had an
inordinate view concerning themselves. They would have
agreed, "We're just a group of God's grasshoppers." The
only difference was that they saw more. They saw God.
What do you see?

When you read through the life of our Saviour, you come
to the statement, "He did not many mighty works there [in
Nazareth] because of their unbelief" (Mt 13:58). The diffi-
culty of the problem was no hindrance; it was the refusal
of the people to believe that He was who He claimed to be—
the Son of God. With us, I believe "faith" is often figuring
what God can do without embarrassment and then asking
Him to do it. But we do not put Him in a bind. We are
afraid to ask Him to do the impossible, because there are so
many problems.

A third principle, I believe, is that God uses a man who does not focus his attention on his ability but rather on his availability. But you say, "I don't have much." My friend, you have all that God intended you to have. "But I can't do much." You can do all that God wants you to do. If you continue to focus on your ability or lack of it, God will never use you. I read in 1 Corinthians 4:2: "It is required in stewards, that a man be found faithful." Not brilliant, not gifted, not spectacular—faithful. The longer I study the life of Elijah, the more I am convinced that what James said of him is true. He was a man of like passions as we (Ja 5:17). He was an ordinary man who lived an extraordinary life. That is his greatest claim to distinction.

Have you ever wondered what goes through the mind of a professor before a class begins? I'll tell you. I have often sat there at my desk and looked at a student and thought, *Lord, what are You going to do with him? How will he ever make it?* I remember one student I had a number of years ago. He slept through most of my classes. He might as well have slept through all of them. How he graduated, I'll never know.

After graduation he took a church up in Canada. The church was 123 years old, and at the end of 123 years of existence it was smaller than when it was first organized. Nineteen pastors in a row had walked away from it as hopeless. And he took the pastorate. I thought, *Well, that's par for the course. He doesn't know enough not to take it.* And he moved into this church, but what was more important, God moved into his life. And dramatic, divinely supernatural things began to happen. Wherever I went, I would hear about this man and his work. One day he wrote me a letter and said, "I understand you're coming up in our area. I'm going to be gone for a little vacation. I'd love to have you preach to my people." I wrote back and said, "I'd love to preach for you. I'd like to see this thing firsthand."

When I arrived at the church, the first thing I noticed was they had begun a building program for expansion—the first new building in 123 years. The sanctuary was so crowded that when I got up to preach I had to give my seat to a man who had been standing. After the service one of the deacons came up and said, "Well, that's pretty good preaching, son." Then he added, "By the way, have you ever heard our preacher preach?" I wouldn't dare tell him I taught him homiletics.

I went back to the seminary with a new lease on life. What am I doing? Erecting a monument to mediocrity? Absolutely not. But I have been at the seminary long enough to learn that brilliance is sterile unless it is coupled with commitment. Does God use a dull tool rather than a sharp one? I do not think so, except that oftentimes the sharp one is not available.

I want to say something that I believe needs to be said. You may have deep-seated inferiority feelings, and the devil has implanted them in your mind. You say, "My, it must be wonderful to be able to preach, to be able to teach in a seminary and multiply yourself." It is. But I only preach and I only teach for one reason: God has gifted me to do it, and I would prostitute the gifts were I not to use them. I never chose these gifts. Nobody ever told me to go to a Christian bookstore and pick this one and this one and this one. God sovereignly bestowed these gifts upon me and upon the other men who are serving Him. And He sovereignly bestowed you with a gift. Don't despise the gift. Your problem is not your ability. Your problem is your availability. When we get to heaven, there are some people who are going to compel some of us who have sustained a public and dramatic type of ministry to step down lower

while they move up higher, because it is required of a stew-
ard, not that he be brilliant, not that he sustain a public
ministry, but that he be faithful in the ministry to which
God has called him.

4

ELIJAH IN COMMUNICATION

IF YOU WERE ASKED to choose a pattern for your prayer life, it is unlikely you would select Elijah. "After all," you might quite reasonably argue, "Elijah was a mighty prophet of God, and I am not. Elijah was a mighty worker of miracles, and I certainly am not." Somehow we have managed to wrap Elijah in a mantle of supernaturalism, with the result that he is unapproachable. He's in another league. But it is not thus that the New Testament remembers him. James 5:17-18 is a highly instructive and illuminating passage of Scripture.

Let me remind you of two things concerning James. In the first place, the epistle of James has more to say about the doctrine of prayer than any other New Testament epistle. The book is drenched with this doctrine. Secondly, James was nicknamed by the early church "Camel knees," so calloused were his knees from incessant praying. When the Holy Spirit wants to teach us the doctrine of prayer, He selects a practitioner, not a theorist. Doctrine is dynamic. Truth is designed not to satisfy your curiosity but to overhaul your experience. But the question nags: Who was it who motivated "Camel knees"? Who turned him on? Who was his pattern?

Verse 17 provides the answer. Out of all of the possibilities, we read "Elias [Elijah] was a man subject to like passions as we are, and he prayed earnestly. . . ." The Word of God does not say, "Elijah was a mighty prophet of God, and he prayed." It does not say, "Elijah was a mighty worker of miracles, and he prayed." It says, "Elijah was a man of like passions." He was cut from the same bolt of human cloth. He had problems, he had perplexities, he had fears, he had doubts, he had frustrations. But he prayed. That's what made him different. That's why "Camel knees" selects him as his paragon for prayer. I believe the New Testament is saying to us that if Elijah is like us in our passions, we may be like him in our prayer. With this biblical backdrop, let's turn to 1 Kings 18, where we see Elijah in communication. We have viewed Elijah in confrontation. We have seen him in concealment beside a drying brook. We have seen him in conflict, in the dramatic action on Carmel. Now we focus our attention on him in communication.

This is certainly not the first time we read of his prayer life. Elijah had prayed that it might not rain. Prayer preceded his encounter with King Ahab. On Mount Carmel, it was prayer that brought down the descending fire. Now, the descending flood.

There are three characteristics of Elijah's prayer life which I trust the Spirit of God will weave into the fabric of our experience. First note in verses 41 and 42 the earnestness of his prayer.

Now mark a relationship. God had promised that it would rain: "And it came to pass after many days, that the word of the LORD came to Elijah in the third year, saying, Go, shew thyself unto Ahab; and I will send rain upon the earth" (18:1). If God promised to send rain, why pray? Prayer is the hand of faith that translates promise into performance. God not only ordains the end, He also ordains the means. It is not a question of coming to a reluctant God in an attempt to persuade Him to do what He really does not want to do in the first place; it is a matter of coming to God with a consciousness that we are dependent individuals. Prayer is the realization that your need is not partial, it's total. Shortly after I became a Christian, someone wrote in the flyleaf of my Bible this couplet:

> When I try, I fail.
> When I trust, He succeeds.

There is a world of theology in that couplet. The Christian life is not a matter of trying, it is a matter of trusting. It is a recognition that the believing life is not difficult, it's impossible, apart from supernatural invasion.

Verse 41 tells us: "And Elijah said unto Ahab, Get thee up, eat and drink; for there is a sound of abundance of rain." I want to stop here for a moment to anticipate something. We are going to read in a subsequent verse that there were no clouds in the sky. How can you hear a sound of abundance of rain when there is not a cloud in the sky? That's the ear of faith. The ear of faith hears when you cannot see.

"So Ahab went up to eat and to drink. [Note the contrast.] And Elijah went up to the top of Carmel; and he cast himself down upon the earth, and put his face between his knees" (v. 42). The text mentions the posture, I think, not because this is to be the pattern but because the posture is outward evidence of inward earnestness. You remember our Lord in the Garden of Gethsemane prostrated Himself on the ground when He cried, "If it be possible, let this cup pass from me: nevertheless, not as I will, but as thou wilt" (Mt 26:39). His position was a reflection of the attitude of His heart.

James says, "He prayed earnestly." This can be quite

literally translated, "He prayed in his prayer." That's a good thought. Very few of us do that.

Isn't it refreshing to listen to a new convert pray? Not long ago we led a man to Christ through our home Bible class ministry. He came to know the Lord on Thursday evening and in the follow-up session that night we said, "The purpose of this class has been fulfilled in your life. It's designed to lead you to the Saviour. We would encourage you now to come to our church, where you can build on this foundation." So he showed up Sunday morning. The pastor announced that we would have an evening service. This man didn't know enough to stay home, and he showed up. In the evening, the pastor announced that we would have Bible study and prayer meeting on Wednesday. Again not knowing enough not to come, he showed up.

Before the prayer session, he turned to me and asked, "Do you think they'd mind if I prayed?" I said, "Of course not. That's what we're here for." "I know," he said, "but I've got a problem. I can't pray the way you people do." I said, "Friend, that's no problem. Thank God for that." But, you know, after a while, he'll learn the clichés and the jargon and he'll be able to say prayers like the rest of us.

A number prayed, and finally I put my hand over on his thigh to encourage him. And I'll never forget his prayer. He said, "Lord, this is Jim. I'm the one that met You last Thursday night. Forgive me, Lord, because I can't say it the way the rest of these people do, but I want to tell You the best I know how. I love You, Lord. Amen." And he ignited the prayer meeting. We were doing a fantastic job scraping the Milky Way. He prayed.

Someday I'm going to write a book on things my children have taught me about theology. A good many years ago now, a scholar was visiting in my home. He happened to come over the mealtime and our family worship time, so I invited him to join us. My children were quite small then, and in typical childlike fashion, they thanked Jesus for the tricycle and the sandbox and the fence. I could tell that our visitor could scarcely wait to get me into the living room.

He said, "Professor Hendricks, you don't mean to tell me that you teach in a theological seminary and yet you teach your children to pray for things like that?" I said, "I certainly do." Then I continued, "Do you ever pray about your Ford?" I knew he did; he was riding mostly on faith and fabric. "Of course," he said, "I certainly do." "Well," I answered, "What made you think your Ford was more important to God than my boy's tricycle? Do you ever pray for protection?" He said, "Brother Hendricks, I never go on the highways but what I pray for protection." I said, "That's what my boy is thanking Jesus for when he thanks Him for the fence. That fence keeps out those great big dogs on the other side!"

Do you know what our problem is? Most of us are educated beyond our intelligence. It's refreshing to have a new convert move into our midst, or a child who in simplicity and earnestness of heart cries out to God. God delights to react to the earnestness of a believing heart.

Now notice in verses 43 and 44 the second characteristic of Elijah's prayer life—the expectation of his prayer. If you underline three statements in three verses, you'll see the story of an answer to prayer. In verse 43, underline the statement, "There is nothing"; in verse 44, "There ariseth a little cloud"; in verse 45, "There was a great rain." Nothing, a little cloud, and a great rain. And the key? Elijah prayed expectantly. He "said to his servant, Go up now, look toward the sea. And he went up, and looked, and said, There is nothing." He sends the servant again, and he comes back—nothing.

The next statement should be translated, "And he said seven times, Go again, Go again, again. . . ." My friends, most of us would have thrown in the towel a long time before this. Suppose Elijah had stopped on the sixth time? But in expectant faith, he sends the servant out to scan the skies because he is looking for something. If you expect nothing, you will be seldom disappointed.

I mentioned before that there is a great deal of humor in the Bible. Acts 12 is another choice case in point. Verse 5: "Peter therefore was kept in prison: but prayer was made without ceasing of the church unto God for him." God answers their prayer. "And when he [Peter] had considered the thing, he came to the house of Mary the mother of John, whose surname was Mark; where many were gathered together praying" (v. 12). For what were they praying? His deliverance. "And as Peter knocked at the door of the gate, a damsel came to hearken, named Rhoda. And when she knew Peter's voice, she opened not the gate for gladness, but ran in, and told how Peter stood before the gate" (vv. 13-14).

Do you get the picture? This little girl looks out through the hatch: "Good night! It's Peter." She's so excited, she forgets to open the door. She runs back. "Hey, Peter's out there." And did they stand to sing the "Hallelujah Chorus" or "Praise God from Whom All Blessings Flow"? No, they said to her, "You're mad." But she was persistent, and she constantly affirmed that it was so.

Can't you visualize the scene as this dear girl says, "Look, I saw him." "No, not Peter. You're seeing things." She would not be put down with that. So they came up with a more profound theological answer: "Oh, well, then it's his angel." They weren't praying for his angel to be delivered. But fortunately the answer to their prayer kept knocking. Peter continued knocking, and if I know Peter, about this time it must have been awfully hard. And when they finally opened the door and saw him, "they were astonished" (v. 16). That's the most mild translation I can think of. A more literal translation would be: "They were dumbfounded—knocked out."

Now before you crawl all over them, suppose somebody came to you today and said, "You know what you've been praying for for twenty-two years?" "Yes, sir. It's been the great burden of my heart." "You have the answer." "I what?" "The Lord answered your prayer." "Don't put me on." "No, your loved one received Christ as his Saviour." "No, you must have somebody else in mind. Is his name Bill?" "Right. He's saved." "Let me see him. I can't believe it."

Oh, may Elijah's tribe increase. "God said it will rain. In fact, I can hear it. Go look for it." "Nothing." "Go look again." "Nothing." "It's coming. Look." And it came.

My wife and I began a procedure I would strongly recommend to any parent. When our children came along, my wife and I took a little looseleaf notebook, and on one side of a page we wrote, "We ask" and on the other side, "He answers." I wouldn't trade anything for this little book in terms of what it enabled me to teach my children about prayer, to teach them different aspects of expectation.

With Elijah, and often with us, there is a clear-cut yes. God said this, that's what He does. What an exciting thing for a child.

We have a lovely family in our community. The father felt God was compelling him into vocational Christian work. So he sold his business at a loss and entered the work to which the Lord had called him. And things got rather rough financially.

One night at family devotions, Timmy, the youngest of

four boys, asked, "Daddy, do you think Jesus would mind if I asked Him for a shirt?" "Of course not," answered his dad. So they wrote in their little prayer-request book, "Shirt for Timmy." Mom added, "Size seven." You can be sure that every night Timmy saw to it that they prayed for the shirt. For weeks they prayed for it—every night.

One day the mother received a telephone call from a Christian businessman, a clothier in downtown Dallas. He said, "I just completed our July clearance sale. Knowing that you have four boys it occurred to me that I have something you might use. Could you use some boys' shirts?' She said, "What size?" "Size seven." "How many do you have?" He said, "I have twelve of them."

What would you do? Some parents would take the shirts and stuff them in the bureau drawer and make some casual comment to the child. Not this enlightened family. That night, as expected—"Don't forget, Mommy, let's pray for the shirt." "We don't have to pray for the shirt, Timmy. The Lord answered your prayer." "He has?" "Right." As previously arranged, brother Tommy goes out, gets the shirt, brings it in, and puts it on the table. Timmy's eyes are like saucers. Tommy goes out, gets another shirt and brings it in. Out, back, out, back, until he has piled twelve shirts on the table, and Timmy thinks God has gone into the shirt business. There's a boy today by the name of Timmy who still believes that there is a God in heaven who is interested enough in a boy's needs to provide a shirt. Do your kids know that? Do you know that in an affluent society?

Sometimes we have had to write "No" in the answer column. Have you come to appreciate with expectation the Lord's no? This is just as much an answer as a yes. My wife and I prayed for two additional children and God appeared to answer that prayer until the time of their birth. They were both born dead. I can still remember coming home and finding my four kids at the door calling, "Hey, Dad! What is it, a boy or a girl?" And I took them over to our little divan and got our little book out and wrote "No" in it.

You will communicate more in one experience like this than in twenty dozen sermons on the subject of prayer. You are coming through at the level at which the child can understand. The problem often is whether we get the message.

Sometimes we are expecting by waiting. Some of those things on that list have been there ever since we started. One of them is the salvation of my father. My father is a retired military officer. Shortly before his retirement, he flew down to Dallas to see us, and of course my kids were so excited. "Granddaddy's coming. We hope he'll wear his uniform." When he appeared in the doorway of the plane in his uniform with all the varicolored ribbons, my youngest boy took off. When my father got to the bottom of the ramp, he threw his arms around him, and just as I caught up with them, I overheard him say, "Hey, Granddaddy. Do you know Jesus yet?" My father said, "No, son, I'm afraid I can't say I do." "Well, you will pretty soon, 'cause we're praying for you." When my father comes to know Jesus Christ as his Saviour, and I am convinced he will, I am equally convinced it will be the product of the faith of my children who have consistently and expectantly prayed for his salvation. Have you been praying for many years, perhaps for the salvation of a loved one? May I encourage you on the authority of the Word of God to go to the brow of the hill again and look. My Saviour said, "Keep on asking and ye shall receive. Keep on seeking, and ye shall find. Keep on knocking and it shall be opened to you." But ask and seek and knock with expectancy.

In verses 45 and 46 I want you to underscore the third characteristic of Elijah's prayer life: the effect of his prayer. "And it came to pass in the mean while, that the heaven was black with clouds and wind, and there was a great rain" (v. 45). There is a twofold effect described in this passage. There is, first of all, the effect of his prayer upon the land. This was no light trickle. This was no soft summer shower, enough to moisten the land but not to satisfy the drought. This was a great rain that broke the prolonged drought. May I say in passing, we are living in spiritually arid conditions. We are surrounded by desert, and God is still looking for a man or woman who is able to bring down the refreshing rain, to break the spiritual drought.

But I also read, in verse 46, that there was a great effect upon this man: "And the hand of the LORD was on Elijah; and he girded up his loins, and ran before Ahab to the entrance of Jezreel." Elijah himself emerges from the experience with a new dynamic: The hand of God was upon him. I cannot think of any greater testimony than this. That's the secret. The hand of God was on him because he knew how to lay hold of the throne of God in prayer.

There is a principle here that I would remind you of: Great praying brings great blessing. Elijah's prayer was great, not because of its language, not because of its length, and certainly not because of its loudness. It was great because it was earnest, it was expectant, and it was invested in the living God.

But it is a dangerous thing to pray. Elijah had learned that. He prayed that it might not rain. The answer to his prayer constituted a drying brook. The disciples learned that. The Lord said, "There's no problem in the harvest; the problem is a shortage of laborers and I want you to pray about it" (see Mt 9:37-38). The interesting thing is that the ones He asked to pray about it were the very men He pressed into service (chap. 10).

When I was a boy I heard Dr. L. L. Legters, a great Bible teacher of the last generation. Frankly, I do not remember very much of what he said, but I have never forgotten an illustration he used. He said that on one occasion when he was pastor of a church, he was walking down the street with fifty dollars in his pocket and he met a missionary home on furlough. The missionary said, "Dr. Legters, I think it's providential that we met. We're having an urgent prayer meeting at the church. We'd love to have you join us." Dr. Legters was a somewhat brusque individual, and before they went to prayer, he said, "Now, let's not pray out of ignorance. Let's pray out of intelligence. Exactly what is it that you need?" "Well," the missionary said, "we have an urgent financial need. We need fifty dollars." "Fine. Let's pray." They went all the way around the circle, and when they got through, one of the missionaries said, "I don't feel that we've really laid hold of the Lord in this. Let's pray some more." Around they went the second time. The third time around, Dr. Legters said, God spoke to him: "Legters, what about the fifty dollars in your pocket?" So he stopped a woman right in the middle of her prayer. "Hold it. God answered your prayer." Dr. Legters put his hand down in his pocket, pulled out the fifty dollars and put it on the table. I can still remember his long, bony finger pointing as he said, "Ladies and gentlemen, it's a dangerous thing to pray."

It still is. Don't ever pray unless you want to get involved. Don't ever pray unless you are personally committed, because the answer to your prayer may demand a beginning with you. James also said it. "Ye have not, because ye ask not. Ye ask, and receive not, because ye ask amiss" (Ja 4:2-3). You ask without earnestness, without expectation.

I want to ask you a question I have been asking myself for some time now: How do you account for the fact that the one area in your Christian experience in which you are constantly bombed out is your prayer life? My friends, that is not an accident, that's the product of cultivation. The older I become in the faith, the more impressed I am with the subtlety of Satan. He always fogs in the area of the crucial, never the trivial. Satan does not mind your witnessing, as long as you don't pray. Because he knows, if you do not, that it is far more important to talk to God about men than to talk to men about God. Satan does not mind your studying the Scriptures, as long as you don't pray, for then the Word will never get into your life. Then you will simply develop a severe case of spiritual pride, and he loves that. Satan doesn't mind your becoming compulsively active in your local church or in some other form of Christian work, just so you do not pray. For then you will be active, but you will not accomplish anything.

The gospels record only fifty-two days in the life of our Lord. Mark 1 tells of one of the busiest recorded days in His life. It was a day crowded with the performance of miracles, with teaching, with healing. No one except a person who has sustained a public ministry has any idea of the drain of people upon an individual in terms of physical and emotional energies. Now look at verse 35: "And in the morning [the morning after the busiest recorded day in the life of our Lord], rising up a great while before day, he went out, and departed into a solitary place, and there prayed." If Jesus Christ, who had unbroken fellowship and communion with the Father, needed to pray, what must my need be? What must your need be? But so high on His priority list was intercourse with the infinite God that after a busy day of service, He rose a great while before day and went to a solitary place to pray.

The work of God today in many areas is languishing, not for lack of divine power but for lack of human prayer. You fight, you war, you bicker, you complain, you scheme, you do everything in the world, James says, but you have not because you ask not.

5

ELIJAH IN CRISIS

WHILE WAITING FOR MY FATHER in his office at the Pentagon some time ago, I picked up a military journal and began to read a fascinating article by Gen. Douglas B. MacArthur, entitled "Requisites for Military Success." He stated four such requisites.

First, there must be morale, a will to win. There must be an esprit de corps. There must be a cause worth dying for. Second, there must be strength. An army must have capabilities in terms of adequately trained and well-equipped personnel. Third, there must be an adequate source of supply. Life lines must be kept open.

The bulk of the article was devoted to the fourth: In order to win, an army must have a knowledge of the enemy. And General MacArthur made this statement: "The greater the knowledge of the enemy, the greater the potential of victory." He traced this principle through military history, beginning with General Joshua and ending with the North African campaign in the second world war where Rommel was finally defeated because of the successful work of counterespionage.

This principle has its parallel in the spiritual realm. Paul knew that, for he told the Corinthians that he did not want Satan to gain an advantage over them (see 2 Co 2:11). And then he adds the reason: "for we are not ignorant of his devices." We are not in the dark as to how the enemy operates. And the greater the knowledge of the enemy, the greater the potential of victory.

In 1 Kings 19, I believe, we find a case study in the strategy of Satan. If I were to give a topic sentence to this chapter, I would write across it: "Victory always makes us vulnerable." There is something about victory that elates, that takes you off your guard, that leaves you wide open to the disparaging arrows of Satan. In chapter 19 it is a short distance from the top of Carmel to the bottom of the valley of despair.

The thing I appreciate about this record is its realism. It is confirming proof of the inspiration of the Scriptures. When God paints a man, He paints him wart and all. He tells the story as it is. From the standpoint of the narrative, it would have been much nicer, much less threatening, to have ended the story at the end of chapter 18. But this would have been contrary to fact. Paul reminds, "Let him that thinketh he standeth take heed [stop, look, listen] lest he fall" (1 Co 10:12). Where? At the very point at which he thinks he's strongest. That's the point at which he is most vulnerable.

Chapters 18 and 19 of 1 Kings are sharply contrasted. The point of Elijah's greatest strength in chapter 18 is the point of his greatest failure in chapter 19. Let's examine this exposé of the devil's devices, for he is still employing the same traps, and he is much more experienced now.

The first trap is found in verses 1-3: the danger of looking at circumstances.

Ahab came home rather late that night. It had been a long and discouraging day. He hoped that Jezebel had gone to sleep. Perhaps he stepped into the palace silently with his shoes in his hand. Suddenly he heard that all too familiar voice, "Ahab." "Yes, dear. I thought you had gone to bed." "No. I couldn't wait to hear you tell me what happened. You look weary." "Yes, I'm very weary." "Would you like something to eat?" "No, thanks. I lost my appetite." "Well, sit down and have a cup of coffee." So she served him some Jezebel java.

Then Jezebel began to ask some rather pressing questions. He tried to change the subject. "Who do you think will win the Samaritan Series?" "Ahab, you're evading the issue. What happened?" And we read in verse 1: "And Ahab told Jezebel all that Elijah had done, and withal [he saved the worst till last] how he had slain all the prophets with the sword."

And then we read, "Then Jezebel sent a messenger unto Elijah, saying, So let the gods do to me and more also, if I make not thy life as the life of one of them by tomorrow about this time. And when he saw that, he arose and went for his life, and came to Beersheba [120 miles south of Jezreel], which belongeth to Judah, and left his servant there" (vv. 2-3). Until now, the only thing that had filled Elijah's vision was Jehovah. Now he is looking through the wrong end of the telescope and his perspective is greatly distorted.

This is always true in the spiritual realm. You remember (Mt 14:22-33) Peter and the other disciples were out in a boat and they looked out over the starboard side and saw what, at first, was a horrible sight: "Why, it looks as if someone's walking on the water." They were scared to death. But then the Lord spoke and they recognized Him. Peter, in his characteristic fashion, said, "Lord, if it's You, bid me come to You." The Lord said, "Come." And now Peter's problem began: stepping over the side of the gunwhale and letting go. I can see him gingerly taking off across the water, and Philip and Andrew are bug-eyed back in the boat watching him go. Finally Andrew hollers out, "Hey, Peter, watch that wave." And he begins to sink. Then Peter prays what is in many ways the most significant prayer in the New Testament: "Lord, save me." (It is also the shortest prayer. If he had prayed like some people do, he would have been twenty feet under.) And the Lord reached down and lifted him out of that watery cavern. How do you think Peter got back to the boat? I'm quite convinced the Lord didn't carry him back; he walked back. I'm equally confident he kept his eyes on the Lord. The moment you and I begin to take our eyes off the source of our courage, we lose it. The moment you take your eyes off the only adequate one, the only one who can protect you and provide for you, you're going to slip on a spiritual banana peel. You're going to sprawl in the faith.

In the book of Philippians, the apostle Paul says, "Rejoice in the Lord alway; and again I say, Rejoice" (4:4). I used to read this and think, *My, what wonderful words.* One day I asked myself, "Where did Paul say them?" He didn't say them in the Statler-Hilton, he said them in a foul-smelling Roman prison. We used to sing a song in America years ago —"Oh, what a beautiful morning . . . everything's going my way." Paul sang, "Oh, what a beautiful morning, everything's going in the opposite direction." That is the kind of rejoicing I want: rejoicing in the midst of reality. This is not happiness, which simply depends on happenings, but rejoicing, which depends on reality.

I have often wondered if Elisha learned this lesson from Elijah. In 2 Kings 6:15-17 we read: "And when the servant of the man of God [Elisha] was risen early, and gone forth, behold an host compassed the city both with horses and chariots. And his servant said unto him, Alas, my master! How shall we do? And he answered, Fear not: for they that be with us are more than they that be with them. And Elisha prayed, and said, LORD, I pray thee, open his eyes, that he may see. And the LORD opened the eyes of the young man; and he saw: and, behold, the mountain was full of horses and chariots of fire round about Elisha." Did Elijah teach Elisha that which he learned in this experience: Don't fasten your eyes on circumstances; you're doomed for a fall. "Greater is he that is in you, than he that is in the world."

I see in verse 4 a second danger to which we are constantly exposed: the danger of praying foolishly. Elijah, not satisfied to go one hundred twenty miles south, "went a day's journey into the wilderness, and came and sat down under a juniper tree: and he requested for himself that he might die; and said, It is enough; now, O LORD, take away my life; for I am not better than my fathers." Single-handedly he took on 850 prophets, but one woman said, "I'll get you," and he ran. "Lord, I've had it. I'm turning in my prophet's badge."

The longer I examine this, the more I think there is a touch of the hypocritical in Elijah's prayer. Whenever you have distorted perspective, you always become dishonest, even in your praying. I don't think Elijah wanted to die. If he had wanted to die, he did not have to travel 120 miles south. All he had to do was to make himself available to Jezebel. She'd be delighted to accommodate him.

Have you ever thanked God for the blessings of unanswered prayer? I sometimes think of the moronic things I have asked God for and I'm so glad He never answered them the way I expected.

Prayer is not asking for what *you* want; it is asking for what *He* wants. One of the first verses of Scripture I ever committed to memory was Psalm 37:4: "Delight thyself also in the LORD; and he shall give thee the desires of thine heart." I can still remember as a young person running that through my mind and saying, "Is that really true? If I delight myself in the Lord, you mean He'll give me anything I want?" That's right. But my problem may have been the same as yours: My occupation was with the desires of my heart, not with the delights of the Lord.

When I was a boy in Philadelphia, I courted a lovely young lady who is now my wife. I lived in northeast Philadelphia and she lived in southwest Philadelphia. We couldn't have been farther apart. It took me an hour and three quarters to go from my home to hers. I had to take a trolley car, a bus, a subway train, and another trolley car. I can still remember storming out of the front door of my home with my grandmother after me: "Howard! Come back. You have to do the dishes." "I'm awfully sorry, Grandma. I don't have time to do the dishes. I've got to go see my girl." And I would get on a trolley car and a bus and a subway train and another trolley car and go all the way across town—to do what? Dishes! And don't feel sorry for me; I cannot even to this day think of anything more delightful than doing dishes in the presence of my wife. Her delights are my desires.

This is exactly what happens in the spiritual realm. His will becomes your will. His way becomes your way. His word becomes your word. And when you are occupied with His delights, then by that strange spiritual metamorphosis, they become your desires. When you come to God in prayer, you pray, "Lord, not what I want, but what You want. Even if it means death at the hands of a Jezebel." Better to die at the hands of a Jezebel in the will of God than to be comfortable and secure in a place outside God's will.

There is a third trap that is becoming higher on my priority list these days because I believe it is higher on the priority list of the enemy. This is the danger of neglecting physical and emotional needs. We are living in a pressurized society, and you cannot **escape the impact of that society.** Christians are subject to emotional and to physical problems just like other members of the human family.

Some time ago we had a very gifted student at Dallas, but unfortunately he lost his perspective in this area. He'd whack away on his sleep at night so he could study more to prepare himself for the Lord's work. And he got it down to six hours. Then he whittled it to five. When he finally got it to four hours a night, he was elated. He kept telling his wife, who couldn't share the excitement, that now he had to spend only four hours a night in sleep and could spend the rest of the time studying the Word and preparing himself for Christian ministry. It took twenty of us at the seminary finally to get hold of him and to get him to professional/help. When his wife, who came to see me for counsel, went to see the psychiatrist, a man of God who was on our seminary board and taught at a nearby medical school, the first thing he asked was, "Mary, what do you do for relaxation?" "Well," she said, "we love to fish." "Wonderful," he said. "When's the last time you went fishing?" She told me later, "Professor Hendricks, it was as if he had pulled back the curtains and suddenly the problem became so transparent." But I'm afraid it's not so transparent to many Christian workers and many Christian laymen who are overly active, supposedly in the Lord's work. This student wanted to cut down his time for rest and relaxation so he could get into a constructive ministry, but he will never, humanly speaking, come out of the institution in which he is found.

I got off a plane for a week of meetings in a church pastored by one of our graduates. This man's wife hurriedly took me off on the side while he went to get my bags, and she said, "Professor Hendricks, while you're here, I wonder if you can help my husband. He is constantly active. He spends no time in rest. He is not recouping his strength and his energies, as you often exhorted us to do. I'm afraid he's going to crack up. He's averaging about four to five hours of sleep a night." A few days went by and we were driving along in the car, and I said to him, "How come you don't smoke?" "How come I don't smoke?" "Yes, I've been here all week and I noticed you don't smoke." He said, "Professor Hendricks, my body is the temple of the Holy Spirit." I said, "That's wonderful, that's very good thinking. Is that also the reason you are prostituting your body with four to five hours of sleep a night?"

It's amazing how spongy our view of the body, the temple of the Holy Spirit, is. We show wisdom in respect to smoking: "My body is the temple of the Holy Spirit. Why put it in the grave prematurely?" By the same logic, why put yourself in the grave prematurely because you are burning the candle at both ends and all along the line?

Beginning with verse 5 is a beautiful picture of the grace of God. "And as he lay and slept under a juniper tree, behold, then an angel touched him, and said unto him, Arise and eat. And he looked, and, behold, there was a cake baken on the coals, and a cruse of water at his head. And he did eat and drink, and laid him down again" (vv. 5-6).

Just think of it—God sent an angel on that mission of mercy thousands of light-years to prepare a meal for His servant. The angel awakens him. Elijah eats and, from sheer exhaustion, goes back to sleep again.

"And the angel of the LORD came again the second time, and touched him, and said, Arise and eat; because the journey is too great for thee" (v. 7). What journey? A journey out of the will of God. You may be out of God's will, but you are never out of His concern. He graciously, tenderly seeks to throw blocks in your way to prevent certain things and to provide for other basic needs that you have.

"And he arose, and did eat and drink, and went in the strength of that meat forty days and forty nights unto Horeb the mount of God" (v. 8). Horeb is more than 200 miles south of Beersheba. So—120 plus 200—it is over 320 miles from where Jezebel said, "I'm going to get you," till Elijah finally stops running.

Someone says, "Don't you know it's better to burn out than to rust out?" This is spiritual nonsense, for that's not the option. It's not a question of burning out or rusting out, it's a question of living out. And that takes the balance of the ministry of the Holy Spirit.

I have often told students who come to see me for counsel, "What I think you really need is a good night of sleep." Did you ever wake up in the morning with a severe headache? It's amazing how unspiritual you feel. I have made it a practice never to make a critical decision when I have a headache, or when I am weary. One good night's rest restores perspective. And God gave Elijah the basis of some perspective He wanted him to have when He revealed Himself.

The last trap I want to lay before you is found in verses 9-10—the trap of feeling you are indispensable: "And he came thither unto a cave, and lodged there; and, behold, the word of the LORD came to him, and he said unto him, What doest thou here, Elijah? And he said, I have been very jealous for the LORD God of hosts: for the children of Israel have forsaken thy covenant, thrown down thine altars, and slain thy prophets with the sword; and I, even I only, am left; and they seek my life, to take it away." "Lord, I'm the only one left, and if they take me, what will happen to Your cause?"

I wonder how many great works, founded under the direction of God, have folded because of one so-called indispensable man? I'm thinking of one Christian organization which was greatly used of God. It was founded by a man of faith and vision who developed it and built it, but he couldn't let go of it. Not only was he its founder and its developer, he was also its undertaker, for he buried it. It is basic to spiritual growth and usefulness that we realize no man is indispensable to God; he is only an instrument. God wants to use you, but the danger is that when He does use you, you begin to think you are the one doing it rather than He. I am convinced that periodically God removes an individual in order to convince us afresh that this is not our work but His.

A young man was dead drunk on a destroyer in Pearl Harbor the morning the Japanese air force struck. In the providence of God, his ship was not hit. Subsequent to that experience he came to know Jesus Christ as his Saviour in a servicemen's center in Honolulu. After the war he finished college and then came to our seminary, was graduated and became a naval chaplain. During a ministry I had in the islands, it was my privilege to have fellowship with him. What a thrill. He held three Sunday morning services in the chapel. And at each one there were more than three hundred men to present the gospel to. He invited a large corps of servicemen to come home with him for dinner. After the meal, we sat around in the living room, and for three hours they plied me with questions. In spite of having to compete with first-run movies which had been shipped to Honolulu so the servicemen could see them first, and which cost just a dime, the chapel was packed to the doors for the evening service. And these young men were hearing the gospel and being taught the Word. Men from bases on the other side of the island would drive clear across the island in order to get into a Bible study taught by this chaplain. I was scarcely back in Dallas when I received a telegram that this young man had been killed. He'd gone over to Guam to dedicate a servicemen's center that he had been instrumental in starting. As the plane was taking off the edge of the runway after he had dedicated the building, it dropped into the jungles. It took three days to find the wreckage.

When I got that message, it was like being hit by a two-by-four. He left four children—barely born, two, four, six. Being a father of four myself, my heart went out to his wife. I sat down to write her the most difficult letter I have ever written, and yet the most instructive to me. I said, "Carol, all things work together. God has underlined that little word *together* in my mind. Not in isolation, but together for good." I thought of all of the chaplains that I had met, many of whom had no concern for spiritual things in terms of the Word of God, and here was one man with zeal, and he was the one taken away. I think it was then that God began to teach me that you do not measure a life in terms of duration. You measure it in terms of contribution.

Suppose Jezebel had snuffed out the life of Elijah? It is altogether possible that this move might have galvanized those seven thousand prophets of Jehovah in the cave. Who are we to judge? No one is indispensable in God's service.

You'll remember the rest of the story. God reveals Himself through various spectacular and dramatic means, but it is finally in the still, small voice that He gets through to Elijah. God wanted to teach the prophet, and you and me, that He not only speaks in the spectacular, He also speaks in silence. He not only speaks in His glory, He also speaks in the grime.

Another great man who had an effect on me was Dr. Harry Ironside, who came to our seminary on so many occasions. I came to appreciate the refreshing down-to-earthness of his spiritual life. I remember one day I could not drive him to where he had to go for the night, so I tried to get a substitute. When I introduced this fellow to Dr. Ironside, I said, "Maybe this young man will take you there, Doctor." He asked, "Would you take me, son?" The young man said, "Well, Dr. Ironside, I'll have to pray about it." And I can still remember Dr. Ironside saying, "No, never mind. If you pray about it and God tells you to take me down there and we get down there and God tells you not to bring me back, I'll be hung." In subsequent reflection on that occasion, I asked Dr. Ironside, "What do you think of a lot of the teaching about spiritual life?" I'll never forget his response: "I think it's wonderful, if you have a lot of time and a lot of money." It took me a long time to understand what he was saying.

Do you know the kind of spiritual life I have come to appreciate? That's the kind that works in the home of a woman with four small children, three of whom are sick in one night. If spiritual living works there, that's what I need, because that's the kind of life I am living.

Have you learned the glory of the grind? To be on the mountaintop is tremendously exciting. But to be in the marketplace, to be in the office, the shop, the home, and there to live distinctively for Christ—that's what I need. That's what God offers to me and to you. But there are many traps en route, and the greater the knowledge of the enemy, the greater the potential for victory.